VIOLA

MOVIE FAVORITES

Solos and String Orchestra Arrangements
Correlated with Essential Elements String Method

Arranged by
ELLIOT DEL BORGO

Welcome to Essential Elements Movie Favorites! There are two versions of each selection in this versatile book. The SOLO version appears in the beginning of your book. The STRING ORCHESTRA arrangements of each song follows. The supplemental CD recording or string orchestra PIANO PART may be used as an accompaniment for solo performance. Use these recordings when playing solos for friends and family.

ISBN 978-0-7935-8420-8

HAL•LEONARD®
CORPORATION

7777 W. BLUEMOUND RD. P.O. BOX 13819 MILWAUKEE, WI 53213

00868021
2nd Edition

CHARIOTS OF FIRE

VIOLA
Solo

Music by VANGELIS
Arranged by ELLIOT DEL BORGO

FORREST GUMP - MAIN TITLE

(Feather Theme)

VIOLA
Solo

Music by ALAN SILVESTRI
Arranged by ELLIOT DEL BORGO

From APOLLO 13

APOLLO 13
(End Credits)

VIOLA
Solo

By JAMES HORNER
Arranged by ELLIOT DEL BORGO

T E JO N DUNBAR T EME

VIOLA
Solo

By JOHN BARRY
Arranged by ELLIOT DEL BORGO

00868021

From the Universal Picture E.T. (THE EXTRA-TERRESTRIAL)

THEME FROM E.T.
(The Extra-Terrestrial)

VIOLA
Solo

Music by JOHN WILLIAMS
Arranged by ELLIOT DEL BORGO

00868021

From the Universal Motion Picture JURASSIC PARK

THEME FROM "JURASSIC PARK"

Composed by JOHN WILLIAMS
Arranged by ELLIOT DEL BORGO

VIOLA
Solo

00868021

MCA MUSIC PUBLISHING

From THE MAN FROM SNOWY RIVER

THE MAN FROM SNOWY RIVER
(Main Title Theme)

VIOLA
Solo

By BRUCE ROWLAND
Arranged by ELLIOT DEL BORGO

MISSION: IMPOSSIBLE THEME

By LALO SCHIFRIN
Arranged by ELLIOT DEL BORGO

VIOLA
Solo

00868021

From the Paramount Motion Picture RAIDERS OF THE LOST ARK

RAIDERS MARCH

VIOLA
Solo

Music by JOHN WILLIAMS
Arranged by ELLIOT DEL BORGO

00868021

From AN AMERICAN TAIL
SOMEWHERE OUT THERE

VIOLA
Solo

Words and Music by JAMES HORNER,
BARRY MANN and CYNTHIA WEIL
Arranged by ELLIOT DEL BORGO

MCA MUSIC PUBLISHING

00868021

STAR TREK® THE MOTION PICTURE

VIOLA
Solo

Music by JERRY GOLDSMITH
Arranged by ELLIOT DEL BORGO

CHARIOTS OF FIRE

VIOLA
String Orchestra Arrangement

Music by VANGELIS
Arranged by ELLIOT DEL BORGO

00868021

From the Paramount Motion Picture FORREST GUMP

FORREST GUMP-MAIN TITLE

(Feather Theme)

VIOLA
String Orchestra Arrangement

Music by ALAN SILVESTRI
Arranged by ELLIOT DEL BORGO

APOLLO 13

(End Credits)

VIOLA
String Orchestra Arrangement

By JAMES HORNER
Arranged by ELLIOT DEL BORGO

MCA MUSIC PUBLISHING

00868021

From DANCES WITH WOLVES

THE JOHN DUNBAR THEME

VIOLA
String Orchestra Arrangement

By JOHN BARRY
Arranged by ELLIOT DEL BORGO

THEME FROM E.T.
(The Extra-Terrestrial)

Music by JOHN WILLIAMS
Arranged by ELLIOT DEL BORGO

VIOLA
String Orchestra Arrangement

00868021

From the Universal Motion Picture JURASSIC PARK

THEME FROM "JURASSIC PARK"

VIOLA
String Orchestra Arrangement

Composed by JOHN WILLIAMS
Arranged by ELLIOT DEL BORGO

00868021

MCA MUSIC PUBLISHING

From THE MAN FROM SNOWY RIVER

THE MAN FROM SNOWY RIVER

(Main Title Theme)

By BRUCE ROWLAND
Arranged by ELLIOT DEL BORGO

VIOLA
String Orchestra Arrangement

From the Paramount Motion Picture MISSION: IMPOSSIBLE

MISSION: IMPOSSIBLE THEME

VIOLA
String Orchestra Arrangement

By LALO SCHIFRIN
Arranged by ELLIOT DEL BORGO

RAIDERS MARCH

VIOLA
String Orchestra Arrangement

Music by JOHN WILLIAMS
Arranged by ELLIOT DEL BORGO

00868021

From AN AMERICAN TAIL
SOMEWHERE OUT THERE

VIOLA
String Orchestra Arrangement

Words and Music by JAMES HORNER,
BARRY MANN and CYNTHIA WEIL
Arranged by ELLIOT DEL BORGO

MCA MUSIC PUBLISHING

STAR TREK® THE MOTION PICTURE

VIOLA
String Orchestra Arrangement

Music by JERRY GOLDSMITH
Arranged by ELLIOT DEL BORGO

00868021